# The Future of
# Network Marketing

The Future of
Network Marketing

Published by Les Editions du Saint-Bernard, 278 Avenue Coghen,
B - 1180 Brussels, Belgium.
Tel: +32-(0)75/45.76.65

Printed in United States

ISBN : 2-9600090-5-3
Registration of copyright in Belgium (Dépot Légal en Belgique):
November 1996 - D/1996/7252/6

Paul and Corinne
Dewandre

# The Future of
# Network Marketing

# Contents

# Preface

*When a friend invited us to a network marketing opportunity meeting several years ago, what we heard interested us greatly. We discovered that this type of marketing was not new, but it was, they said, the opportunity of the future. And we were there at the right time.*

*We asked ourselves why this distribution method, which had been seldomly used in the past, would develop now with such great success. We studied financial reports on the network marketing industry and noticed that some companies using this technique showed unusual growth.*

*But does this growth alone prove that network marketing will develop in the future to the point where, in 10 years' time, it will be a popular means of distribution?*

*This book contains our reflections on these issues.*

*We hope that it will help people answer their own questions.*

# Introduction

# Network Marketing:
# Short-Term Fad or Long-Term Trend?

We are going through a period of economic and social evolution. Our work environment is changing, and the media speak of an "economic crisis." While numerous enterprises are laying people off and others are filing for bankruptcy, new companies are being born every day. Some have seen surprising growth and realized great profits.

Product innovation for many companies created a business boom. Such breakthroughs take several forms. First is the development of new products. Sony's Walkman, for instance, brought the company incredible revenues.

Alternatively, one can achieve the competitive edge through a product's technological improvement. The word processor is a good example. When it became popular, the mechanical typewriter industry disappeared almost overnight. While companies that made typewriters had to lay off their personnel and close their doors, the manufacturers of the new technology prospered.

Innovations in production itself have allowed a number of manufacturing firms to reduce the cost of making their products. The automation of production lines ensures a high return on investment and permits these firms to reap greater profits than their competitors.

Changing the location of the production site is another form of innovation that has seen enormous growth in recent years. Delocalizing has permitted many firms to reduce production costs. Finding the labels "Made in China" or "Made in Brazil" no longer surprises anyone. Production costs are lower in regions where worker hours and warehousing are less expensive. Transportation costs have also gone down significantly in the last few years, making it possible to manufacture quality products abroad at a better price.

Another innovation involves product distribution. Innovations in this area constitute one of today's major challenges for commerce. We see new means of distribution developing, such as mail order, TV home shopping, direct selling and even selling through the Internet. Firms are looking for better ways to serve their customers.

One distribution technique that more and more people are talking about is network marketing, a distribution method that first appeared in the 1940s in the United States. Over the past 10 years in the United States and Japan, the turnover (i.e., the ratio of  goods sold to average number of goods in inventory) of some firms using network marketing has skyrocketed. The number of companies that include this form of distribution in their strategic approach goes up every year.  In fact, some independent distributors created networks so large that in only five years they could retire.

In recent years, this trend has also become evident in Europe and other parts of the world. Some countries, such as Great Britain, Germany, China and Australia, already boast large networks, whereas other countries like France have felt the effect of this movement much more recently.

Is network marketing truly the wave of the future? Network marketing occasionally—and often unfairly—elicits negative press. And sometimes this skepticism is reflected in our own beliefs. As with any new concept, we are often torn between two emotions when we first come into contact with network marketing. First a great enthusiasm: "Yes! This is exactly what I want to do. It seems fun, lucrative and simple." But after sharing this enthusiasm with a friend, coworker or spouse, warning signals start to flash: "That's an illegal pyramid! It's a sect! You are going to go broke!"

What can we make of all this?

Can network marketing develop in our marketplaces? Is it a real opportunity or a fad that is going to fade out just as quickly as it appeared? How does this distribution method compare to other means of distribution that are also developing, such as direct selling, mail order and TV home shopping?

Are criticisms based on ethical principles? Do they seek to protect the consumer from poor-quality products or the distributors from themselves? Or maybe what the detractors are voicing is simply a classic resistance often encountered at the beginning of any change. Aren't these dismissals founded on fear of the unknown—a fear caused by lack of information?

Can we predict the future of this type of business? Is it reasonable to think that network marketing will soon be as well known as the franchise? Are network marketing distributors visionaries, pioneers or madmen?

There are answers to these questions. Even if we cannot predict the future with certainty, we can see that the trends of tomorrow are taking shape today. If we analyze the trends that mark our daily lives and compare them to the principles by which network marketing functions, we can decide whether or not network marketing will suit our new working and purchasing habits.

In order to see the future of network marketing, we must answer the following questions:

— What are the trends of tomorrow?
— By what principles does network marketing work?
— Does network marketing match tomorrow's trends?

Only after we have closely examined these angles can we then assess its viability in the business community.

✳

# Part I

# What Does the Future Hold?

*To predict is difficult, especially the future.*
Pierre Dac

# Chapter 1
# Knowing the Trends of Tomorrow

Is there a formula for predicting the future? This question must be answered by every firm that wants to innovate. If it wants to create a new product, will consumers like it? Will new packaging please them more? Will a different type of advertising have more impact? As Faith Popcorn writes in her Popcorn Report, "No one knows (exactly) how the future will feel or unfold, but the trends are taking us there with a force that's almost tangible."

Every day we are confronted by an incalculable amount of information from a wide variety of sources: television, radio, advertisements, newspapers, books, journals, store windows, fashion in the street, the new architecture of buildings, new cars, conversations that we have or have overheard and so on. We record this information subconsciously and hardly pay attention to it, but we can also regroup, dissect, analyze, compare and discern general trends from it.

The 1950s was typified by cars with chrome bumpers, the modern kitchen, nylons, and the jukebox. The 1960s saw feminism and the Beatles, the Pill changed morals and the miniskirt created an uproar. In the 1970s we had the oil crisis, bohemianism, communal life and the disco craze. The 1980s was the "greed-is-good" decade, with its yuppies, aerobics, personal computers and general obsession with fitness and material acquisition.

## The 1990s . . . and Beyond

The trends of today are difficult to define. The lack of hindsight makes the exercise less easy, but words like environment, cocooning, nature, purity, simplify, family values and ethics appear to be especially characteristic of our time.

Some futurologists have studied the question in depth with interesting conclusions. Faith Popcorn founded and directs a company called BrainReserve. Nicknamed the "Nostradamus of Marketing," BrainReserve is an American firm of marketing consultants with a worldwide reputation. Giants of industry, including Coca-Cola, Gillette, Toyota and AT&T, employ its method of "analysis of the conformity to trends." Faith Popcorn and her team use brainstorming to identify 10 major trends that mark daily life in the United States.

For the last 15 years another American, John Naisbitt, has published a trend report titled *Megatrends* that sells for $15,000 a copy. From analysis of both print and electronic news media, and the frequency of recurring themes in the news, the Naisbitt group has defined the overall trends that influence our economy. These trends were initially apparent in North America but slowly appeared in other parts of the world such as Western and Eastern Europe, Asia and the Pacific Rim.

Other futurologists and analysts also deserve consideration. Alvin Toffler, the author of the famous book *The Third Wave*, explained as early as 1980 the arrival of a new age marked by the computer. His latest study, *Creating a New Civilization: The Politics of the Third Wave*, shows the impact on everyday life from having enormous amounts of information (and misinformation) at our fingertips.

In *Unlimited Wealth*, Paul Zane Pilzer "shapes things to come." Denis Waitley, in *Empires of the Mind*, redefines the ways to lead and succeed in a knowledge-based world, the world of the twenty-first century. Other studies such as Credoc in France, the Statistische Bundesamt in Germany and English economist Charles Handy's *Beyond Certainty* are worth reading too.

By using the same techniques as these futurologists, we have identified the major trends that are influencing the way we purchase and the way we work.

✷

## The First Trend: The Return Home

The most important trend of our time is The Return Home, which began in the 1980s. Faith Popcorn uses the word "cocooning" to describe this trend. She predicted as early as 1970 that Americans would retreat to the safety and comfort of their homes and park themselves in their easy chairs with remote control in hand and a telephone close by to order pizzas. Now she has gone even further. She speaks about "burrowing," adding the fear of going out into an ever more terrifying world.

This trend is not only happening in the United States but globally. All of a sudden we think of nightclubs and discos as passé! Now we want to relax in a hot bath after working hard all day, followed by a cozy evening of TV and conversation at home. We order a take-out meal or prepare a frozen dinner in the microwave, then settle in to watch a video delivered from the local store or a pay-per-view event beamed into our home via satellite. At-home services even include hairstylists and car washing. Dry cleaners come to pick up suits and bring them back clean the next day, and banks offer transactions by phone or computer.

We think twice before leaving our homes to fight city traffic jams, search for parking spaces and risk the danger of the streets just to subject ourselves to noisy, smoke-filled restaurants and overworked waiters. After all, why go out when we can eat in the security and comfort of our homes?

With the desire to enjoy the company of our children and pets, we get into our new station wagon and set off to take a long walk in the woods on a Sunday. The "cocoon home" has been extended to the "cocoon car." Anti-lock brakes and front and side airbags comfort us with the idea of cushioned security.

## The Second Trend: The Wary Buyer

Thoughtless, reckless money spending is now part of the past. We demand quality at a reasonable price. We read labels down to the fine print and scrutinize deceptive advertising. We have become cautious consumers.

We buy consumer magazines and read comparative test reports. We then ask the opinions of friends and coworkers to see if the results from magazines are corroborated by other's opinions. Informational television programs that target the Wary Buyer and review products are becoming increasingly common.

When we do buy, we want an after-sale warranty, and we will only buy from a supplier we have confidence in. For this reason, companies are setting up toll-free help lines to inform customers about the quality and origin of their products.

✳

## The Third Trend: Personalized Selling

In today's market, we demand "personalized selling" to meet our unique expectations. We claim our right to be different and to have our own identity. We no longer want uniformity but demand customized service. As Denis Waitley writes, "Today, customers come first."

In the past our options were limited. If we wanted a chair, for example, we had to choose from what was available on the showroom floor. Today we can choose the style we want, as well and the pattern and quality of the fabric, to suit our personal tastes and needs.

With each purchase, we demand quality, beauty and practicality. When we buy a car, we can select from a seemingly endless combination of options such as exterior color, upholstery fabric and pattern, air conditioning, manual or automatic transmission, central locking, and so forth. Customized features for our rolling cocoon!

Service is just as important. We choose our suppliers not only by the quality of their products but also by the services that accompany the sale, both during and after. We like to be recognized by our suppliers. A little birthday card or a personalized letter with respect to our tastes and habits makes a big difference. The French car manufacturer Peugeot has created a repair service for emergency breakdowns for their own vehicles as well as for others' in several European countries. Often it is the extra services that help us choose between one supplier and another.

## The Fourth Trend: Nature and Technology

We are becoming increasingly aware of the opinion that our crazy race to succeed is poisoning us. The unending routine of  rushing to the office and back home again has made many folks reassess their well-being.

In the 1970s, people started to think about living a healthier lifestyle. Some even went so far as to leave behind their business suits and executive-level positions to raise sheep in the country. But this exodus was limited by a lack of technology. It was hard to make a living selling cheese or to effectively advertise a farmhouse that had been converted into a bed and breakfast.

Then the technological innovations of the Computer Age started to have an impact on our lives. Fax machines, PCs, better telephone services, cheap air travel, bullet trains and expressways have all contributed to making the world a smaller place and are invaluable to the entrepreneur. With them, it is now possible to keep in touch with business without always having to be in a downtown office.

So what keeps people in the city? Work, school, cultural attractions . . . but in time these will all be accessible from the home. Couples often dream of working together from home. Parents wish they could spend more time with their children but still earn a living. Technology can improve the quality of life and gray the distinction between home and workplace.

Telephone services, including conference calling, will continue to improve in the next few years, and costs will go down. It is reasonable to expect that, in five years' time, most systems will send visual images as well as sound and we will be able to have face-to-face telephone conversations.

Soon families will be able to live in rural areas and the children will still receive a full education by video-conference. Having been raised on Nintendo and interactive CDs, this will seem quite normal to them.

Should we be afraid that human contact will disappear? Just ask anyone who lives in a city and who has spent time in the country, or vice versa. Can we really say that human relationships in the city are "warm"? Have we forged friendships while waiting in traffic jams or on the subway? Neighborly readiness to lend a helping hand is legendary in small towns, yet we barely say "hello" to the person living in the apartment next door.

As John Naisbitt and Patricia Aberdene note in *Megatrends 2000*, "In the United States, for the first time in 200 years, more people are moving to rural areas than urban. In the Northeast, West, Great Plains and Southwest, everywhere, people are moving from cities and suburbs to rural areas. They are abandoning cities for quality-of-life reasons: low crime rates, comparatively low housing costs, recreational opportunities and, perhaps most of all, a return to community values."

## The Fifth Trend: The Quality of Life

Parallel to the trend to retreat from a hectic life is this fact: we no longer want to, nor can be, employed in the same job by the same employer until the end of our days. In the 1960s, we went to school, then upon graduation, dedicated the rest of our lives to some large company. It was so easy! Our place was guaranteed. Benjamin Braddock, the young protagonist in *The Graduate*, voices the dilemma of that period: "I am worried about the future." Yet a family friend addresses the dilemma with a single word. "Plastics," the man says.

What does life in a company now offer us? Steady pay, certainly, but at what price? Often we are tied down by the stress of working hours that we cannot choose—not to mention infrequent promotions and pay raises. We no longer enjoy our free time because we only use it to "decompress" from the exhausting life we lead. We would love to spend more time with our family and wonder whether this crazy race is worth the effort.

For some of us, the race ends abruptly. We are laid off and begin the even more dispiriting task of finding a new job. The newly unemployed are engulfed in deep depression. The tacit contract that binds us to our companies—"I give you my time, you give me the security of knowing that I will be paid tomorrow"—is no longer renewed. Firms have had to realize that it is no longer economically feasible to keep personnel on "for better or for worse."

We no longer want to feel like we are on the verge of catastrophe. The best way to avoid it is to create our own business. No more fixed working hours, no more nasty rivalry with a colleague for the same coveted position. ("So who will be left behind in the traditional corporate structure? Who knows?" asks Faith Popcorn. "The unsecured, maybe, and the meanest.")

To work for oneself does not mean working less. On the contrary, self-employed people are often more relentless and dynamic. After all, they put their future in their own hands.

We are fed up with dependence on handouts. We can no longer count on the government to bail us out. Is there no one to protect us? We soon realize that we can protect ourselves. We have already begun to do this with regard to our health. We believe less in "miracle cures." We now take the first step on our own by paying more attention to the needs of our bodies by eating better and exercising regularly.

Further, the advice of experts is no longer so esoteric. We read about what interests us in specialized magazines and from in-depth studies. Articles that explain scientific discoveries in common terms are readily available. Magazines for the general public contain pointed articles about medical and scientific discoveries and the most recent philosophical research… we are becoming our own experts.

We have reclaimed a new physical and moral health and want to believe in ourselves. We know that we need to work on our subconscious to overcome our limitations. Yesterday, only "crazy" people went to psychiatrists. Today, without hesitation healthy people consult psychoanalysts, psychologists, support groups or relationship-skill therapists. We no longer fear letting our desire for better mental health be known. Books on psychology and personal development are flying out of bookstores.

One after another, companies have started to organize personal development seminars. The original idea was to improve employee relationships (and, hence, performance) in order to achieve the best-possible communication among team members. The demand for training has increased so dramatically that a new industry of qualified consultants has developed to supply this niche market. The most common form of training involves goal-setting and time management, but other areas include public speaking, assertiveness, memory skills and teamwork. These types of training are so popular now that more and more people are taking them on their own initiative.

We have realized in the last few years that we have forgotten some fundamentally important things. Money is no longer of primary importance. The quality of our relationships with those around us—both at home and at work—is an increasingly high priority. We want a full, happy and healthy life.

## The Sixth Trend: A Search for Ethics

"Yesterday profits were earned through expediency. Today profits are earned with integrity," writes Denis Waitley. We are reclaiming our values. We buy products that respect the environment or that are made by manufacturers who support humanitarian causes. We look for sincere products that give us the feeling of being a "moral" consumer. When in 1995 the newly elected French President Jacques Chirac decided to do more nuclear tests in Polynesia, French products were boycotted by many consumers throughout the world. In England, aggressive TV spots against French wine appeared, while manufacturers of French beauty products started putting stickers on their product's packaging, declaring their stance against nuclear testing.

The quest for profit has its limits. We feel tricked by greedy politicians and businesspeople who have money and power. Our leaders are held accountable to the nation. Transparency has replaced corruption. Governments can no longer afford to break the rules.

Certainly we have to do something that puts money in the bank, but we want that something to be honorable. To succeed at the expense of others is no longer fashionable.

We look for real relationships based on respect for one another. According to Naisbitt, in the coming era, we will pass "from being the helped out, to the individual making it on his own." A time that will be marked by "the triumph of the individual."

\*

# Chapter 2
# The Consequences of Today's Trends

Today's trends manifest themselves in everyday life, but for the most part, they influence two changing facets of our environment: our buying and our working habits.

## New Buying Habits

Companies have to adapt to our new requirements. We do not want to run around to a lot of different stores anymore. Let them come to us! Catalogs, telephones, television, a visiting salesperson—all allow us to select what we like at home quietly and with less hassle.

Small stores do not fulfill tomorrow's trends. Finding parking places, lugging around purchases, going from store to store . . . we still have to do this sometimes, but we no longer prefer to shop this way. It is much easier to pick up the phone, order what we want and pay by credit card.

Large stores do not fulfill tomorrow's trends either. Long lines at the check-out counters or cashiers who would rather talk to each other than with the customer do not match our desire to Return Home. Today's large, impersonal stores do not correspond to our need for personalized service. They are anti-custom made.

Some modern grocery stores have begun to respond to our expectations. Customer service is getting better. Debit and charge cards are appearing, as are specialized and gourmet food sections and catering services.

We still go to the grocery store regularly , but how long will we continue? Only until another way to do the grocery shopping is available—one better suited to our needs. There are already some companies that will shop for you and make home deliveries. Some grocery stores even catalog their merchandise, take your order by phone and send out your choice by mail. This practice is destined to become more popular. Faith Popcorn thinks that someday we will only go to grocery stores for diversion. They will still be the center of other attractions, including the bustling of daily life, games and the taste-testing of new foods.

The suppliers of goods must find ways to serve us at home, to know us personally, to serve us affably and to guarantee reliable after-sale services. In fact, a growing number of companies are employing such methods.

## Non-Store Retailing

Generally, "non-store retailing" encompasses all sorts of alternative types of purchasing, such as direct selling,, mail order, TV home shopping and network marketing. These alternative means of distribution have already been thoroughly developed. They permit a more personal approach to selling. Not surprisingly, each one of these methods has seen phenomenal growth in recent years.

## Direct Selling

Direct selling can be either one-to-one between a representative and client in the client's home or in the form of a product party or showcase. Many companies operate in different parts of the world with traveling salespeople, on either a salaried or independent basis, who offer goods and services directly to consumers. The personalized contact and service that the salesperson provides for the client meet the demands of the market.

## Mail Order

Another form of non-store retailing is mail order. Clients purchase from home something they have seen in a catalog, a newspaper ad or a promotional mailer. Orders are placed by mail, telephone or computer, and delivered often by regular postal service, but sometimes by a service maintained by the mail-order company. This type of selling is not new, but it is getting more and more popular.

Mail order conforms to trends such as The Return Home and Personalized Selling. Following the latter trend, some mail-order companies distribute the same catalog under different names to capture a wider target market. Mail order also conforms to the trend of The Wary Buyer, who takes time to choose and compare.

Nowadays, mail-order companies use the most recent technological innovations at their disposal: automated wrapping systems, sophisticated computer networks and voice mail systems to optimize their efficiency.

### TV Home Shopping

One of the first TV home shopping programs was broadcast in Italy in 1974. They have been a success there ever since.

In 1985 in the United States, a national network began broadcasting TV home shopping 24 hours a day. The expansion of the cable TV has contributed to the success of home shopping networks. American TV home shopping is now sent by satellite to other countries, and local TV home shopping is developing here and there.

Also, the development of Web TV—the technology by which people can access the Internet through their television sets—will probably bring about a decisive breakthrough in home shopping. With Internet-capable television, people are able to view, order and pay for merchandise right from their TV screens.

### Network Marketing

Network marketing is the most recent form of direct selling. The basic principle is that a large number of people each carry out a few individual sales. Distributors advertise the product and are compensated accordingly by the manufacturer. Consumers benefit from being able to shop at home and by being sold merchandise by a trusted friend. This method of distribution and its principles are analyzed in greater detail in the second part of this book.

From the entrepreneur's point of view, network marketing offers a new means of selling that pays close attention to the trends of The Return Home, Personalized Selling and The Wary Buyer. As an added bonus, this industry also permits motivated people to start their own distribution companies.

In addition, network marketing complements our new working habits.

\*

**New Working Habits**

Our working habits have changed. Working for large companies corresponds less and less to our desire to spend more time cocooned at home, to exercise more control over our lives and to feel more fulfilled. So, what impact does this have on us today?

Paul Pilzer writes that in 1931 a young English student won a scholarship to study in the United States. The student was surprised to find that in a country known for its business opportunities, most Americans preferred to work in large companies rather than as individual business entrepreneurs.

"Why," the student asked, "in a free market economy, would a worker voluntarily submit to direction by a corporation instead of selling his own output or service directly to customers in the market?"

The student was Ronald Coase, who won a Nobel Prize in Economics in 1991. His work of 1931, *The Nature of the Firm,* analyzes the reasons why people stay in large companies.

Even after 60 years, this work is still one of the most frequently cited in contemporary economic research. Professor Pilzer thinks that if Coase researched the same question today, however, he would come to a diametrically opposite conclusion.

In The *Nature of the Firm*, Ronald Coase explains the success of large firms in terms of their ability to reduce "transaction costs" between individuals. He cites an example in which a manager wants to dictate a letter and have it typed. The manager could hire someone for the specific task of typing the letter, but the transaction cost of hiring such an employee for a set time would greatly exceed the value of the work demanded. Interviewing candidates, assessing each candidate's abilities and negotiating a salary would all be an unnecessary waste of time for the manager, who finally decides to type the letter without help.

The interest of large firms has been to reduce transaction costs between themselves and the suppliers who provide services by hiring people with necessary skills on a permanent basis. This limits the number of contract negotiations. Labor contracts are discussed at the time of hiring and thereafter only for possible pay raises. Unfortunately, the firm loses its work flexibility, but it has one advantage: there is always someone available to perform each task. At the same time, the company risks not being able to occupy the employee's time if there is a work slowdown. Employees compromise their independence and the ability to manage their own time in exchange for a regular salary and a stable position.

Meanwhile, as the company grows, it generates expenses in the management of personnel. The larger the company gets, the more difficult it is to transmit information in-house, which results in bad decision-making and, consequently, increased costs. In addition, there are the costs of laying off personnel. These costs have risen enormously with the growth of workers' rights. Coase named all these costs "inefficiency costs."

For Coase, a firm is the ideal size when transaction costs are equal to inefficiency costs; but since 1930, transaction costs have dropped while inefficiency costs are increasing. Indeed, transaction costs that are added to goods and services furnished by a supplier outside the company (i.e., the cost of communication, delivery and accounting) have become so low in respect to the value of goods and services that they are often no longer a major consideration when a business selects a supplier. Likewise, transaction costs such as telephone and fax charges will decrease even more in the future.

Inefficiency costs are now a major burden to large firms. Since the 1960s, due to the inflation that began in that period, employees have become accustomed to annual cost-of-living pay raises independent of their individual job performance.

Many companies who grew too large too quickly have failed. As Alvin and Heidi Toffler summarize it: "The more a company is complicated, the less the left hand is able to foresee what the right hand is going to do. Fissures appear while problems arise that threaten to prevail on the presumed advantages of the mass effect. The old idea that the bigger the company the more likely it is to be well armed is now more and more antiquated."

The cost of employing workers in term of taxes, social security payments and pension funds are a considerable burden to businesses as well. These costs also increase regularly, regardless of the workers' performances.

Often we hear of situations in which two employees of a large firm carry out exactly the same job. One has just been hired; the other has 10 years' seniority. Even if the result of their work is exactly the same, their pay may vary by as much as 50 percent.

According to Coase, however, the main reason for rising inefficiency costs in large companies is the inability to apply new technologies quickly to meet changing needs. Entrepreneurs, on the other hand, can gain the competitive edge because they are flexible enough to avoid these problems.

At the start of the Computer Age, only large corporations had the resources for leading-edge technologies. Now any small business can afford the latest computers and software.

Likewise, in the past only employees of these large companies had the opportunity to work with new technologies. Today the key to success, for both companies and individuals, is to learn to use technology as soon as it is available. The ability to adapt to innovation allows people to pull themselves out of economic crisis. Employees of large firms who are known more for their fidelity than for their ability to innovate are usually the last to learn new skills.

When employees join a company, they go through a training period. What they learn makes them an asset. Over time, they may receive a promotion and an increase in salary. If there comes a time when their value to the company does not increase, yet they still receive pay raises, they can evaluate the situation for themselves. Two risks await: unemployment or the company's bankruptcy!

If resistance to change by the less dynamic employees results in the slow implementation of new technologies, the more dynamic employees will look to escape from the limits imposed on them. They are going to give up less and less of their liberty in exchange for empty promises of job security. An increasing number of these people are deciding to set up their own businesses.

The corporate system is not, however, going to fall apart overnight. It still offers many advantages to employers and employees alike. Some companies will adapt to technological changes and will avoid inefficiency costs by hiring the most dynamic and open-minded candidates from the job market.

According to Faith Popcorn, we will witness a complete transformation in the structure of work:

"Future teams of workers can still meet for conference and lunches, or gossip-and-coffee sessions over the telescreen. The corporate headquarters, though smaller, can still exist to provide offices and conference rooms for team projects, large meeting centers for yearly or twice-yearly 'rallies' and recreation and retreat centers to encourage corporate spirit. Roving secretaries can supply some day-to-day contact."

## The End of Job Security

Our former economic certainties have been swept away by events. Major companies no longer wield the power they did yesterday. No one can guarantee us a job for life any longer. Therefore, it is important that each individual reflect on his or her capacities for submitting to the laws of the labor market. Each individual should considered him- or herself a mini-company composed of one who creates added value for an employer.

We sell our labor, under salary or as an independent, and we are paid for it. The salaried worker sells time to the company that pays the salary. One can also sell one's services directly, at the value assigned. That's what independents do.

In an age where job security no longer exists, it is important that each individual, or mini-company, realizes that he or she must try to diversify and increase his or her customer base. Of course, one can increase one's customer base by selling separate services to several customers. That is why we see more and more people having two or more sources of income: a salary from an in-house company and income generated from work as an independent.

Dynamic people no longer see any future for themselves in large existing corporate structures. They are looking for alternatives. These truly independent people want to have neither their earnings limited nor their liberty compromised. They are moving away from the idea that earnings must be proportional to the number of hours worked.

*

# Part II

# Network Marketing

*Network marketing, yes!  Pyramid selling, no!*
Pascal Clément
Former French Minister

# Chapter 3
# The Evolution of Distribution

The appearance of network marketing as a new marketing technique illustrates that changes occurring in this century have made it possible for the development of new ways to distribute products.

## Distribution: The Opportunity of the Nineties

In the past, production costs comprised 80 percent of the price of a product, and distribution and transportation costs the other 20 percent. Due to the inefficient methods of transportation, there was no choice but to manufacture products in close proximity to their markets. Back then, looking for ways to reduce production costs was most businesses' primary concern.

Now technological innovations permit extraordinary reductions in production costs. Highly specialized machinery has lowered costs associated with labor, and production lines are increasingly automated. In addition, low-cost transportation—most importantly train and boat, followed by truck and air—has allowed delocalization of production sites. It is now easy to produce goods at low cost in distant locations. Even when products are not entirely manufactured elsewhere, often the individual components are manufactured abroad and assembled locally.

Production costs have declined consistently since the 1950s, allowing clients to buy merchandise at significantly better prices. Today's task is not simply to produce a product or service but to reach the consumer.

The success of an airline, for example, is not in the number or type of airplanes that the company owns. The major difference between a flourishing company and one on the brink of bankruptcy is the efficiency of its reservation and ticketing network. The ticket sold is the one accessible to the public through the greatest number of point-of-sale locations.

If an airline underestimates customer volume, the company can always rent aircraft on a temporary basis from specialized businesses and raise production. As production gains flexibility, distribution becomes the most important task in business today.

McDonald's might not make the best hamburgers in the world, but they are found everywhere. The company, therefore, is the most successful. When McDonald's started producing its Chicken McNuggets, overnight the company became the largest seller of chicken in the world. This is the power of distribution.

For a long time, consumers looked to brand names as an indicator of guaranteed quality. Since the 1980s, however, large stores have sold merchandise under generic labels. These stores rely exclusively on their means of distribution to sell products. Their advertising costs disappeared, allowing them to sell products even more cheaply. We now find excellent-quality merchandise, and even luxury items, with generic labels. Chain stores research the types of products that sell best, order directly from the manufacturer and market them to the public at a lower price.

Distribution is one of today's largest areas of potential growth. As Paul Pilzer writes in *Unlimited Wealth*, "Until well into the twentieth century, most of the greatest personal fortunes in America history—fortune like those of the Astors (fur trading), the Rockefellers (oil), the Carnegies (steel) and the Fords (automobiles)—were built on the bedrock of natural resources and manufacturing. In our modern...world, however, the route to wealth has shifted. In the last decade or two, the biggest personal fortunes have all been earned by individuals like Fred Smith (who founded Federal Express) and H. Ross Perot (Electronic Data Systems)—who made their mark by coming up with new and better ways to move goods and share information."

✳

**Distribution Techniques**

Since about 1850, techniques for distribution improved constantly. Village markets were rivaled by small shops. Larger stores (John Wanamaker in Pennsylvania, Harrods in London) and chain stores (Sears, K-Mart) followed. Their success led to supermarkets and warehouse stores that offer similar products at more competitive prices.

At the same time, two other distribution techniques developed: direct selling and franchising.

### Direct Selling through a Representative

Consumers want to buy high-quality merchandise at competitive prices with good service. Salespeople strive to satisfy them. One way of lowering distribution costs while still ensuring the quality of service is to reduce the number of middle-providers in the distribution process. Direct selling techniques can be divided into groups: door-to-door selling, distance selling (mail order by catalogs, telephone services, television), parties organized as product showcases and membership clubs. Overheads, such as storage and high-cost retail locations, are eliminated.

Door-to-door selling has seen its glory days. In the 1930s, delighted housewives bought revolutionary new vacuum cleaners from dapper young men who impressed them with the countless merits of their product. Today's sales representatives would not succeed relying on these methods. With the high percentage of working women, someone is not always at home. Furthermore, we no longer open the door of our cocoon to someone we do not know. We fear thieves casing their next "job."

In other respects, the system of sales by commercial representatives has also developed inefficiency costs, as defined by Ronald Coase. At the heart of that business, there are problems in the management of personnel and the respect of geographical market subdivisions. Furthermore, salespersons who approach work with a great deal of enthusiasm may actually be limited in their potential to expand the business by a superior who does not want to lose his or her own position.

### The Franchise

To avoid personnel problems, some manufacturers have developed the system of franchising. The manufacturer directs the development of a product, its advertising and the development of the retail outlet, but passes on the right to conduct sales to an independent distributor. The basic principle is to promote client loyalty. The customers are assured of the quality of the goods and services that are provided to them, no matter where they are purchased.

Let's take another look at McDonald's. When they became a franchise, they not only selected the ingredients for the food, they also standardized all other aspects of the business. The hats that the cashiers wear are the same everywhere, as is the layout of the children's play area and everything else, from Montreal to Bangkok.

On the other hand, the managers of most McDonald's are independents. They have bought the right to sell McDonald's hamburgers. They take courses in the proper techniques of serving customers so that the quality of service is consistent. McDonald's, the franchiser, only sees a small fraction of the price of each hamburger sold, but because their stores are all over the world, this adds up to a considerable amount of money. The franchisees also stand to make considerable profits, because they have an almost guaranteed success formula.

Franchise holders develop their own businesses by making use of a promising idea developed by the franchiser and its purchasing power. Companies such as Hertz, Benetton, Pizza Hut and many others provide their franchise holders a name, a reputation, advertising, know-how and after-sale service within a contractual time period. To benefit, the holder pays an entry fee and a percentage of its profits. The franchise holder is contractually bound to respect rules aimed at unifying commercial policies, such as the look and decor of the retail outlet, the uniforms of the personnel, supplies, and the use of specific advertising and promotional materials.

\*

Though franchising and direct marketing are both effective methods of selling products, they do have drawbacks. As we'll see in the next chapter, network marketing combines the principles behind both of these methods, taking the benefits of each and avoiding the pitfalls.

# Chapter 4
# The Workings of Network Marketing

Network marketing draws its inspiration from principles taken from both franchising and direct selling. From the franchise, it takes the principle of independent distribution carried out under the wing of the manufacturer. From direct selling, it takes the principle of only one intermediary between the network marketing company and the consumer: the distributor.

By bringing together characteristics of franchising and direct selling, network marketing has succeeded in avoiding their individual drawbacks. Setting up a network marketing business does not require the capital that is necessary to purchase a franchise, and the selling methods of the independent distributor are different from those of door-to-door salespeople and traveling representatives. The newly created role of "distributor" is therefore vastly different from that of people involved in other forms of distribution.

The aim of this chapter is not to look at the nuts and bolts of network marketing. The bibliography of this book contains a list of works that thoroughly investigate the subject.

Instead, here we would like to understand the principles at work in network marketing by examining its broader characteristics.

Peter Clothier defines network marketing as follows:

*"A method of selling goods directly to consumers through a network developed by independent distributors introducing further distributors, with income being generated by retail and wholesale profits supplemented by payments based upon the total sales of the group built by a distributor."*

On one side of manufacturing we have firms who have turned to network marketing to market their product; on the other are people called "distributors" who create their own distribution businesses. Distributors must be introduced by another distributor: a sponsor.

Companies as well known as AT&T, Colgate-Palmolive, Gillette, Philips, Sony and many others supply products to network marketing businesses or even operate themselves through network marketing subsidiaries.

**Word-of-Mouth**

Technically, network marketing capitalizes on the principle of word-of-mouth. When we like a car, a hotel, a restaurant, a brand of whiskey or a new movie, we announce it by telling those around us. When decide to buy a dog or a camcorder, or to go on vacation, we ask the advice of friends and listen to their recommendations with great interest. Our opinions are influenced by people around us. In fact, in *Personal Influence*, Elihy Katz and Paul F.

Lazarsfeld show that 30 percent of our decisions are directly affected by other people.

Most of the time, the business that benefits from this efficient word-of-mouth advertising does not even know that it is going on and cannot thank those who are making it happen. Network marketing companies are able to reward people who use word-of-mouth publicity to recommend a product that they like.

As John Kalench writes in *Being the Best You Can Be in MLM*, "As friends share good news, when you discover a product or a service that gives you some benefit, you have a desire to tell others about it. In network marketing, this is exactly why you get paid. Think of this money as a way for the company to say 'thank you.'"

## A Network of Independent Distributors

Distributors in network marketing have two opportunities. On the one hand, they show and recommend the product. They profit from a margin on the sale (the direct selling principle). On the other hand, for a small annual fee, distributors are allowed to set up their own networks. They profit from the turnover generated (the franchise principle). Payment usually comes directly from the network marketing company, which calculates each distributor's check with the aid of sophisticated computer systems. Distributors are encouraged to dedicate their time and energy equally between these two functions.

## Limited Risk

It is not necessary to invest capital to create a network marketing distribution business. A few demonstration products are all one needs to start. Some distributors may risk keeping a small stock, but the purchase of these products is not obligatory. This makes network marketing a low-risk venture.

## No Boss, No Employees

The network marketing system makes use of a form of total business independence. A small independent business is set up under the direction of one person without subordinates. The distributor's relationship with the sponsor is a relationship of equals. Those who try to direct the members of their network meet with little success. Each distributor must take personal responsibility because success depends on an individual's work.

In network marketing, there are no underlings to carry out the work for you. Therefore, there are no labor-management problems or lay-off payments to calculate, nor vacation pay and replacement workers to take into account.

## A Family Business

A popular way to conduct business for a large number of distributors is to work in families. Married and unmarried couples, fathers and sons, mothers and daughters, sisters and brothers have found myriad ways to work together. This flexible profession is full of possibilities. No formal qualifications are necessary. In addition, stay-at-home moms are often delighted to take part in the business. Even if it is part-time work, they are not limited to stuffing envelopes.

## You Cannot Get By on Your Own

A unique features of network marketing is that one person cannot succeed without helping others to do the same. Profit is related to the success of the people you sponsor. You create a truly profitable business when you succeed in helping many other people to create their own flourishing businesses.

By sponsoring one person, the distributor commits to providing help and information. A new distributor needs support to learn the profession. The system of payment, as it is established, motivates the sponsor to help the distributor who just set up shop.

## Open to Everyone

Network marketing distributorship is open to everyone. It does not matter whether or not you are a college graduate, male or female, young or old. A wide variety of people succeed in building network marketing businesses. Former waiters, secretaries, businesspeople, teachers, doctors, veterinarians, carpenters—all have an opportunity to achieve the great success they desire by working within the network marketing system.

However, not everyone succeeds. At present, statistics show that only 20 to 40 percent of distributors will make it through their first year. Finding the first good people to sponsor is actually more difficult than it seems. Many do not evaluate properly their own will to succeed. Giving up is so easy—even more so because the financial stake is limited.

Not surprisingly, there are characteristics among those network marketing distributors who  make it work. One is a spirit of openness. Also, successful distributors tend to have a positive and optimistic outlook, a willingness to take responsibility for themselves and clearly defined personal goals. They have a sense of purpose in life and high self-esteem. Persistent and adventurous pioneers, they work hard and are able to help people.

## Flexible Time

Most people work in their network marketing businesses on a part-time basis. They are able to take advantage of the flexibility of network marketing in order to manage their time as they wish and to profit from the additional income that this business provides.

It is very easy to begin your own network marketing business by working evenings and weekends to keep it going while working a job with regular hours. When the business is fairly well developed after a year or two (sometimes more, sometimes less), then you can devote all your time to it.

This sort of work offers a flexibility that simply does not exist in the corporate world.

# Chapter 5
# Ethics in Network Marketing

Despite the impressive success of network marketing, the business is only just starting to build momentum. It needs to create a good name for itself by adopting a rigorous ethical code.

The principle of network marketing is highly ethical. Competition is replaced by a commitment to others. Since network marketing is open to everyone, the chance for success is equal for all. Selling is conducted without pressure. However, abuse of the system is possible and must be avoided at all costs.

All distribution methods have their share of corruption. Discount stores have been known to sell products at a loss in order to attract customers, and some franchisers conduct themselves improperly with respect to their franchise holders. But despite these occasional violations, we still believe that most discount shops and franchises are ethical.

Furthermore, legislators have stepped in to regulate new professions and to prohibit abuse. Of course, the law always lags behind the evolution of actual practice. It is therefore essential for the common good of the profession that a code of ethics, dictated from within, is followed by network marketing firms themselves and respected by each of their distributors.

Numerous professions adopt ethical codes that they expect each practitioner of their trade to follow. The deceptive doctor, shady lawyer, corrupt pharmacist and dishonest notary are customarily reprimanded or expelled by their professional regulatory bodies.

Since the profession of network marketing is comprised of groups of distributors, the personal conduct of each distributor has an impact on the industry's image as a whole—bad or good. Even though a regulatory body of network marketing distributors does not yet exist in most countries, each distributor should ensure that basic ethical principles are respected.

## The Direct Selling Association Code of Ethics

Network marketing's roots lie in the principles of direct selling; therefore, it can easily adopt a basic ethical code. Most countries have an established direct selling group, such as the Direct Selling Association (DSA) in the UK or the DSAS in Singapore. These associations are globally represented by the World Federation of Direct Selling Association (WFDSA), based in Washington, DC.

These groups have drawn up guidelines relating to ethical codes that their members must respect. Many network marketing companies are already-formed associations and have incorporated their principles into the contracts that bind them to their distributors. The dishonest distributor who breaks the rules will lose the right to do business.

These associations have created two categories of regulations:

1. Rules of conduct to protect the consumer. These include a genuine product, the availability of detailed and honest product information, a guarantee from the company and quality service, including after-sales support.

2. Rules of conduct for the salesperson and the company. These include recruitment methods, formal written contracts, minimal entry fees, good training and a reliable supply of merchandise.

These general rules of the Direct Selling Code of Ethics are applied to network marketing, but specific rules must be added to the list. These rules are aimed at both the company and the distributor.

# The Company's Ethical Code

### *Small Entry Fee*

The company must ensure that entry fees are proportional to real administrative or training costs involved in creating the distributorship. This participation must not benefit the sponsor in any way. The entry fee should be paid directly to the network marketing company and not to the sponsor to avoid a "pyramid" or "snowball" type of business structure.

## *No Obligation to Buy Stock of Merchandise*

The contract between the company and the distributor should stipulate clearly that there is no purchasing obligation imposed. Otherwise, the sponsor would generate an income purely by signing up distributors, regardless of whether or not retail sales take place.

The new distributor, of course, has an interest in buying demonstration products to help build business. The difference between being "overstocked" and "well-stocked" is difficult to define. It largely depends on the objectives of the distributor and the magnitude of the commitment made vis-à-vis the new distribution business.

The network marketing company may stipulate a reasonable purchase limit of demonstration products. It may restrict investment for the first product order and verify that the first products are actually sold before further supplies are authorized.

## *Obligation to Buy Back Unsold Merchandise*

The company should contractually commit itself to buying back any merchandise that the distributor does not sell. This complements the "no obligation to buy stock" rule. With rare exceptions, this approach does not exist in the world of traditional business, where all merchants incapable of selling their goods simply take a loss. Serious network marketing companies are so successful that they can afford to build this "limited-risk" option into their contractual obligation to distributors. Nevertheless, be sure that the company is stable. If it goes bankrupt, the buy-back guarantee will be useless!

### No Exaggerated Profit from Advertising and Training Material (Cassettes and Brochures)

The network marketing distributor's job is so different from jobs we are accustomed to that a complete training program is required. Manuals, videos and audio cassettes have been designed to help circulate correct information.

Also, network marketing companies often supply distributors with informational materials about the product or about selling techniques, such as the "Distributor's Tool Kit" or "Getting Started Package." The sale of these tools, all very important to know the business, should represent a small part of the revenues of both distributor and companies.

*

## The Distributor's Ethical Code

In order to succeed, network marketing distributors must have a vision and clearly defined goals. They need enthusiasm and a positive mind-set to communicate well with consumers. It is, however, necessary to maintain an irreproachably objective point of view and to allow consumers to form their own opinions. Distributors must obey imperatively a few good-conduct rules, violation of which would do harm to the entire profession.

### Honesty about the Performance of a Product

The network marketing industry, like all forms of commerce, is subject to regulations that forbid misleading advertising and deceptive sales practices. Moreover, suggesting product benefits that are untrue creates a serious problem for the company and for other distributors as well. Word-of-mouth is a two-edged sword. It is great when positive information circulates rapidly, and the quality and advantages of goods or services are widely disseminated; however, negative information can get around with twice the speed and efficiency.

✳

### *Honesty about the Magnitude of the Work*

The network marketing system is almost unique in that there are genuinely no limits to the revenues it can generate. Beyond this honest statement, a new distributor needs to be aware that establishing a prosperous business requires a considerable amount of persistent effort. Much damage is done by novice distributors who assure you that all you need to do is sit back and wait for the money to roll in!

For the most part, a network marketing distributor only begins to see significant returns after two to five years of work. Results depend on personality, quality of effort and level of motivation of the entire team.

Success requires perseverance, self-confidence, action, a positive and optimistic attitude, determination and ethics. This is why the majority of people who think of network marketing as a get-rich-quick scheme will be disappointed and will not make it through the first year.

### Respect of Legal Formalities

The network marketing distributor's profession is of a commercial nature. It is not a job one is "employed" to do, but a chance to create one's own distribution business. Therefore, each country probably will have legal formalities that must be followed.

Obviously, the network marketing distributor's income is taxable and must be declared. To conceal income from the government is not only fiscal fraud, it also tarnishes the image of the network marketing industry as a whole. The sponsor who is helping a new distributor create a business has a duty to emphasize this.

Having said that, some network marketing companies take charge of all or part of the administrative formalities normally carried out by a distributor. This is a great incentive to get started. It is, however, the responsibility of each distributor to verify that all legal obligations have been fulfilled.

✳

If all regulations are respected, network marketing will become what it was designed to be: an excellent means to do business with a small investment and a serious possibility for anyone to begin a new profession. These ethical rules are so important that they have drawn the attention of our lawmakers. Most countries are now adapting their legislation to include this new means of distribution.

# Part III

# Network Marketing
# and Today's Trend

*Consumers and companies have everything to gain
from the development of network marketing.*
Edmond Alphandery
Former French Minister of Economy


*Lost your belief in Big Business?
Start your own small one, based on your expertise.*
Faith Popcorn
*Clicking*

# Chapter 6
# Network Marketing's Conformity to Today's Trends

Network marketing's success is due largely to the fact that it corresponds to the six major trends observed in many parts of the world. Let's look at each one with regard to this method of distribution.

## Network Marketing and The Return Home

Network marketing is a form of direct selling that takes place in the client's home—in the beloved cocoon. It allows for a simplified and pleasant buying experience. We feel security in knowing that we are dealing with a friend who is not trying to take advantage of us. And we are able to profit from a warm contact without opening the door to a stranger. Quite the opposite from the stereotyped idea of a door-to-door salesman forcing his way in and selling things we do not even want.

*

## Network Marketing and The Wary Buyer

We buy with care. We look for good quality at a reasonable price and listen to other people's advice. What are we sensitive to? To the power of word-of-mouth, to what our friends have tried out and what they liked. We feel comfortable buying in an atmosphere of trust, and who would we trust more than someone we have known for a long time?

The network marketing company further supports the efforts of its distributors by setting up toll-free numbers for consumers. They can call a customer service line for answers to questions about a product.

∗

## Network Marketing and Personalized Selling

Network marketing satisfies our desire for personal service; it makes us feel special. To this end, the network marketing company must make sure that after-sales service are impeccable. As consumers, we expect the network marketing company and distributor to resolve any problems that may occur with products we have purchased. The company is well aware that it relies solely on the power of word-of-mouth advertising.

∗

## Network Marketing and Nature and Technology

For those who want to manage their own time and create their own business without taking too many risks, network marketing offers a serious alternative to the corporate world's maddening race to succeed. We can work from home, close to our family. Parents can reconcile the demands of work with the education of their children.

New communication technologies are suited perfectly to the network marketing distributor's needs. Telephones and fax machines are available to everyone. More and more people have VCRs, so most can watch cassettes presenting companies and their products. As airline tickets become more affordable, building distribution networks internationally is increasingly cost-effective.

Network marketing companies rely on powerful computers and sophisticated software programs to handle millions of orders from hundreds of thousands of distributors. Companies bring together the technology of tomorrow in the best way: conference call training and product upgrades are now common in countries such as the United States and Australia. One network marketing leader speaks to anywhere from 5 to 1,000 people at once. In the future, visual conference calling will make this technology an even more powerful tool.

✳

**Network Marketing and The Quality of Life**

We have become our own experts and form our own opinions on numerous issues. We are capable of acquiring cutting-edge information and knowledge in new fields. To learn a new profession that may propel us toward success appears an enriching challenge to us. Our increasing disillusionment with the welfare system strengthens this desire to set our own goals and ways to achieve them.

As a result, many people who get involved in network marketing discover that the personal development they experience helps them in many aspects of their lives. Self-confidence, better listening and public speaking skills, and higher self-esteem are often indirectly acquired as a result of distributing the product or service and developing a network.

With hard work comes the potential for an exceptional income and an escape from the treadmill of traditional business.

*

**Network Marketing and A Search for Ethics**

Because of network marketing's fundamental principles, only those who are willing to help others, improve themselves, work with a strong code of ethics and accept responsibility for their actions will reap benefits. Power-hungry money-grubbers will not get far, as they cannot develop the relationships of trust essential to network building.

# Chapter 7
# Network Marketing and
# New Buying and Working Habits

Network marketing fits current trends perfectly and corresponds to our new way of buying from home through personal contact and guaranteed service. It also allows more autonomous and flexible working habits.

## Network Marketing: Distribution that Suits Our New Buying Habits

Through the distribution process, network marketing fulfills another very important role: customer education, as described by Paul Zane Pilzer in *Should You Quit Before You're Fired?*

The first washing machine was introduced in 1922. It took about 10 years until everyone had heard about this fabulous invention and could find a shop in which to buy it. In 1939, the first black-and-white television sets appeared.

After World War II, new consumer items were invented with increasing frequency. These innovations revolutionized our daily lives. The process of innovation has accelerated to the point where, nowadays, new inventions and technologies show up not every five years, but every five months!

Large "megastores" have experienced phenomenal success in recent years by buying in bulk to reduce costs. They also fulfill another fundamental role: anyone can go to a big store to buy what they want and at the same time see new products. This is still a way many people pick and choose goods. Today, however, people are happier to get the same quality of information without fighting through crowds.

For a long time TV and other forms of media advertising have influenced our perceptions of new products and services, but we no longer buy without question. Nevertheless, advertising is so efficient that costs have skyrocketed, making it a cost-effective tool only for mass-market products.

The shopper who wants more specific information has to look elsewhere: specialized shops and publications, the advice of salespeople (not always accurate in larger stores) and increasingly, advice from friends who are happy with the particular item they bought.

Network marketing satisfies all these criteria, allowing consumers to make purchasing decisions at home based on friendly advice. The distributor's job changes from the role of a salesperson to that of a communicator and teacher who develops contacts and builds rapport.

This leads to a situation where manufacturers increasingly consider the possibility of using existing networks to distribute their products. What better, more rapid, efficient and inexpensive way exists for making a new product known? Word-of-mouth is not only powerful, it guarantees a certain level of truth by its very nature. We are taking charge of our responsibilities, and we are becoming wary consumers. Trickery is no longer tolerated. A bad product or a bad service will not be recommended by thousands of individuals.

\*

## The Network Marketing Industry: A Work Alternative

Why are network marketing companies experiencing phenomenal growth rates during a period of economic crisis, reduced economic growth and frequent layoffs? How can they do this without even incurring short-, middle- and long-term debt?

Network marketing companies succeed because they minimize inefficiency costs and avoid transaction costs by:

— Using independent distributors who work at their own speed, for their own objectives and for their own profits. No bosses, no subordinates—no hierarchy at all in traditional business terms—exactly the kind of system described as a "hierarchy of a network of contacts" by John Naisbitt. These distributors are not held under a contract of employment, with all the associated costs and problems.

— Minimizing the number of actual employees to those who manufacture the product, arrange deliveries and support the registration, payment and queries of distributors.

— Using efficient computer systems that ensure distributors are paid according to the company's marketing plan. Also, the company helps with some transaction costs (such as phone hot lines, product delivery and organization of opportunity meetings and training sessions). Other costs are absorbed by the distributors themselves, who are directly bound to the company, not to each other.

Ronald Coase recommends that a professional organization balance inefficiency costs and transaction costs. Network marketing does this; therefore, the system is stable. Because both of these costs are minimal, the method attains extraordinary results—and the industry is only now starting to gain momentum.

Network marketing also avoids the unfair situations of traditional business where, for example, two workers perform the same job but are paid unequally due to seniority. Similarly, young, dynamic workers do not have to wait for their boss to quit before they can get a promotion. In addition, firing older workers or forcing early retirements when times are hard is unnecessary.

Distributors are paid on the basis of the turnover realized by their group. The company effectively pays for the team development just as much as it does for the retailing of the product. This is why there are no limits to the earnings that a distributor can make.

The opportunity to create a large network is the same for everybody; they all have the same company and the same products. The only variable is the individual and what he or she is prepared to put into the business. It is not uncommon for new recruits to build stronger businesses than their sponsors. As corporations decline, therefore, thousands—even millions— can prosper in a new network marketing professional career.

What about the argument as to whether or not it is a "real profession" or just a hobby for bored housewives looking for a way to make some extra money? This issue arises because there is no prestige in "being accepted" as a distributor. You do not even need an approval of a bank loan. Start-up costs are low. In principle, anyone who seriously wants to create a distribution business can do it. There are no exams or entrance tests. Although some sponsors may dedicate their time only to high-potential candidates, in general, anyone who wants to join is welcomed.

The other side of the coin is that because the opportunity is open to everyone, there is no guarantee of success. This is one of the biggest criticisms of network marketing, yet there are many parallel situations that we readily accept. School, for example, is open to everyone, but not everyone completes it successfully. It is up to individuals to assess their own abilities and working habits and decide if network marketing is for them.

Network marketing is a business that discourages those who have never succeeded in any of their goals because of laziness or other bad habits. In general, it requires people who are (or want to become) self-confident and persistent, and who have a positive frame of mind.

Network marketing does offer an alternative to traditional employment. Anyone unhappy with their situation can learn to be a successful distributor.

✳

# Part IV

# The Future of Network Marketing

*The future isn't what it used to be.*
Yogi Berra

# Chapter 8
# The Speed of Change

Network marketing is a relatively unknown innovation, and therefore, universal acceptance is still to come. This is not surprising. Society has certain ways of dealing with new ideas and change. It is possible, for instance, that your neighbor does not know how to operate a computer, loves to work in the infrastructure of a large corporation, enjoys the hectic life of the big city and has not— and never will— read a book on personal development. Not everyone deals with the evolving world in the same way. Some are open to change and others are more comfortable holding on to tradition. How these patterns are reflected in reactions to network marketing is quite interesting.

## Adopting New Ideas

In 1983, an American economist, Everett M. Rogers, evaluated the time necessary for consumers to accept new ideas. He noted that people react differently to new products and concepts. When a successful product is launched, the level of sales starts small. As more people accept the innovation, sales grow to a peak. They then level off as those slow to change their habits decide to break down and buy the product.

Rogers identified five groups of consumers:

— 2.5 percent of consumers are pioneers and embrace innovation. They try new ideas, take risks and possess a spirit of adventure.

— 13.5 percent are forward-thinking and adapt to changes. Their opinion is respected and they adopt the roles of leaders. At the right moment they accept new ideas but will do so with caution.

— 34 percent are forward thinkers who like innovation but do not have a pioneering attitude. Their dominant characteristic is that they think deeply about their decisions.

— 34 percent are referred to as the "slow majority." These are the skeptics who only accept innovation once it is backed by the weight of public opinion.

— 16 percent are traditionalists and slow to change. Their fear of change and evolution is overcome only when the "innovation" is widely accepted and becomes part of tradition.

✶

## The Psychological Process of Accepting Change

Regardless of which consumer group we may be in, all of us must pass through a series of psychological phases in order to accept a new idea. What differentiates our behavior from one another and makes us a pioneer or a traditionalist is the speed with which we move through these phases. They are:

— Indifference: We pay slight attention to something in the beginning.

— Derision: We react to the innovation with a derisive smile, if not full-blown laughter.

— Opposition: We look for any good reason to justify believing the innovation is impossible.

— Acceptance: We finally find enough evidence to accept the new idea.

— Indispute: The idea is so commonplace, it seems as though it was always there.

Consider the example of private radio broadcasting. It began in France in the 1970s when enthusiasts started transmitting unofficially in a 20-kilometer radius. Few people noticed (phase of indifference).

The pioneering individuals, usually young, became a target of ridicule to their friends (phase of derision). Soon, however, popularity grew, especially among teenagers, to the point where advertisements could be introduced as a source of revenue.

Private radio's popularity gave rise to government intervention, who declared that the airwaves were the property of the State and must therefore be assigned to "serious" radio companies only. This outlawed the independents and resulted in arrests and seizure of equipment (phase of opposition).

In spite of this opposition, the movement grew in strength, and 10 years later, the conscientious public began to accept the idea of privately held stations. Laws were adapted accordingly (phase of acceptance) and independent stations are now common (phase of indispute). Some are spectacularly successful. "Lovin' Fun" on Fun Radio in France, for example, receives up to 40,000 calls daily from young people eager to be on the air. Up to 2.5 million people from several French-speaking countries tune in every night via satellite.

Similarly, microwaves were at first regarded with indifference. Why have a second oven when the first one works perfectly well? Besides, there is little enough space in the kitchen, and it is only a passing fad, anyway.

Then the opposition phase. Aren't these waves dangerous? They probably cause cancer or lead to sterility. Rumors begin to circulate that manufacturers of microwaves are knee-deep in legal battles!

Eventually, more and more people realized the benefits. Now microwaves are part of our everyday lives. In fact, for some frozen products we buy, the microwave is the only cooking method suggested on the box.

Let's look at a few famous historical statements :

> "The phonograph… is not of any commercial value."
> — Thomas Edison, remarking on his own invention
>   to his assistant, Sam Insull, 1880

> "Who the hell wants to hear actors talk?"
> — Harry Warner, Warner Brothers Pictures, 1927

> "I think there is a world market for about five
> computers."
> — Thomas J. Watson, chairman of IBM, 1943

> "There is no reason for any individual to have a
> computer in their home."
> — Ken Olsen, president of Digital Equipment
>   Corporation, 1977

The people talking were not stupid—quite the contrary, they were all considered experts in their fields. But innovation is not obvious at first sight, and it takes everyone time to get accustomed to it.

\*

## The Acceleration of Evolution

From the beginning of time, humanity has been affected by technological innovations. The Fire Age, Stone Age, Iron Age and Industrial Age mark distinct periods of history. Each era revolves around the discovery of a new technology developed over hundreds of years.

The twentieth century has seen significant agricultural breakthroughs. From 1930 to 1980, the number of people involved in this industry was cut in half, while output has increased through the use of modern fertilizers made possible by advances in the chemical industry. And all these changes occurred in the space of two generations! Grandfather retires from his farm, his son works in a chemical company and his grandson repairs computers!

For centuries it had been traditional for a son to follow in his father's footsteps. Some dynasties still exist, producing generations of military officers, lawyers, pastors and bakers, but new professions have appeared in the last few years and changed traditions. Most people now work in sectors that did not even exist when their parents were choosing careers.

Until 20 years ago, starting with a large company implied "a job for life." This concept is completely alien to young people today. The economic climate and desire for variety mean that the average employee will change companies every few years, before—possibly—establishing his or her own.

One of the reasons for this is the speed at which technological progress takes place. As John Naisbitt writes in *Global Paradox*, "Technology is developing at an ever-accelerating rate of speed, with each new technology compounding the speed and capabilities of those that came before."

In this time of creative explosion, it is no wonder that we change our professional direction many times during the course of our lives. Another result of these changes is that we no longer use most of what we learned in school. Who can tell if our own skills will still be marketable in five years' time?

People can change paths to go in whatever direction they want. It is not unusual now for a qualified dietician to become the handler of a sporting goods store. Even a registered veterinarian can become a weather forecaster on television if he really want to! The 1994 Rally champion in Europe was a former ambulance driver. And Arnold Schwarzenegger became an actor after studying chemistry and being a world-class bodybuilder.

*

## Resistance to Change

Throughout history, people have been reluctant to accept change. In the 1850ss during the Industrial Revolution, machines began to take over the jobs of craftspeople and farmers. Mechanical weaving looms successfully increased productivity and improved quality to produce a more regular, stronger fabric. New looms were much faster, too.

Thousands of weavers lost their jobs and revolted, destroying factories and burning warehouses. They saw machines as enemies. The frightened working class perceived the purchase of these great innovations as a personal attack on their livelihood. People went without work for some time, until the most industrious learned how to work with the new machines. These risk takers became skilled laborers, and their lifestyle improved. In a few years, the quality of life improved for everyone, along with a return to full employment.

Today the Information Age is having the same effect. The application of technology once again is increasing productivity. Although we have the impression that computers are replacing humans in professional occupations, we will eventually witness the same trend as in the past. After the fluctuations of change have settled, the result will be an improved standard of living for everyone.

These technological advances also give us much more freedom than we have had in the past. We can be contacted anywhere by phone or fax, and information can easily be stored and managed by computer. Now more than ever we can continue to be professionals while living outside big cities. Who likes spending three hours a day in the car going to and from work? Cities are a perfect example of wasted energy and talent, triggering dysfunctional and disorderly lives for millions.

$$*$$

**Fear of Loss**

Often what holds us back from risking the unknown is the fear of losing what we already have. Just look at the difficulties in adopting any reform. People will demonstrate to keep their rights and to keep things exactly the way they are. This is just as true for large corporations and governments as it is for individuals. However, the fear of quitting a job may result in missed opportunities. To learn to overcome obstacles, it is of primary importance to be self-confident and take the risky options regardless of fears. Courage invites success.

\*

## The Pessimism of the Media

Network marketing is the perfect distribution method to satisfy current lifestyles throughout the world. It is common, however, for it to receive criticism. People form a negative opinion quickly based on a hostile newspaper article and believe network marketing is some type of "scam." But why is the press concerning network marketing so negative? Basically, because the media skews toward negative news.

Over the course of the twentieth century, the media has become so prominent that it is now commonly known as "the Fourth Estate." And what do we see when we read the headlines? What are the leading stories on televised news programs? Catastrophes. Layoffs. Attacks.

The media, like all industries, must obey the laws of supply and demand. Journalists and newscasters alike have a legitimate concern about how many people their work is reaching. Journalists want to please their clients with high circulations, which in turn means increased revenues and higher wages. Obviously, journalist must work to find stories that inform and entertain the public, and in our society, hot news is about catastrophes, scandals and things that are going wrong.

Economic life regularly takes its broad themes from those that we hold dear: layoffs of workers, bankruptcies of companies and high rates of unemployment. When do we hear about workers who find a new job within a month of being fired? More emphasis is placed on the company that goes bust than the company that creates new jobs. If we believe the media, we might imagine our countries' economies to be in a state of crisis. In fact, the majority of us do have a roof over our heads, enough to eat and a great deal more. Our quality of life is probably far superior to that of our grandparents.

Of course, there are homeless people whose misfortune is highlighted by the press every time the nights get cold. But we rarely see articles on former homeless people who have found a home and the means to get by. These people suffered through bad times but made it out the other side.

As French sociologist Gaston Joufroy eloquently writes:

"We always talk about crisis when we live in a time of richness. In this time of richness, dramatic things happen. But should we dramatize them? The media has no educative role, since they prefer to dramatize things."

Good news does not enthrall the public with the same fascination as bad news.

\*

Yet, just as in the Industrial Revolution, when pioneering individuals built solid businesses as a result of their investment in new machinery, it is the people who embrace new technologies who become highly successful tomorrow. We must learn to keep an open mind about new ideas and not reject them out of hand before understanding more about them.

# Chapter 9
# Network Marketing as an Innovation

Network marketing is different from anything we currently know. To understand and embrace it, we must pass through each of the five phases outlined in the previous chapter for the acceptance of innovation.

After some indifference, negative questions come to mind: Isn't this a sort of snowball scam or an illegal pyramid? Didn't the nightly news do a report on the similarities between network marketing companies and religious sects? Won't I lose both my money and my friends?

## Toward a Healthy Ethical Code

These questions are completely justified if the system's ethical code has been ignored. If we have bought a large stock of products and cannot sell or return them to the company, we lose our money. If we try to pawn them off by harassing our friends, we risk losing them, too. If our sponsor enticed us by promising unrealistic profits in the first month by finding five other people to sign a contract, we will see in time that this is all a delusion.

When first introduced, the franchise system was also sharply criticized. Abuse of the system by a small minority of franchisers sowed doubt in the minds of the public. Franchising only started to gain popularity as a strong ethical code was adopted by the entire profession.

Serious network marketing companies already incorporate such ethical codes in their distributor's contracts. Once these rules are in place and effective, network marketing can begin to move from the phase of opposition to the phase of acceptance.

*

## Network Marketing Distributor: A New Profession

As mentioned, network marketing has been in existence since the 1940s but has only really begun to gain popularity since the 1980s. This can be explained partially by network marketing's dependence on technology. Just as Leonardo Da Vinci could not develop the flying machine he invented, lacking a power source not to be invented for centuries, network marketing could not flourish until the Computer Age could support its administration. Today, new technologies permit our society to evolve, and new professions are created every day.

It is not necessary to have studied network marketing in a business school or in the economics department of a university to create a successful distribution network. In fact, most business courses do not even include network marketing in their curricula.

Network marketing distributors come from all walks of life and all professions. They have an equal chance of success. Everything that needs knowing can be learned by the new distributor and, in time, be passed on to future recruits. In this way, information and skills can be duplicated throughout a network.

Professional salespeople also must learn new skills, as they are often the people who have the most difficulty adapting to the network marketing mind-set. Door-to-door selling tricks produce disastrous results when applied to network marketing. Information passed by word-of-mouth transmits negative opinions as well. A sponsor has the responsibility to help new distributors make sales by sharing the product just as they would share happy experiences. The industry's image depends on it.

\*

**Network Marketing and the Process of Acceptance**

The third phase of the acceptance process is opposition. It is not surprising, therefore, that some people cry "scandal" as soon as they hear about network marketing.

Let's look at a parallel example. When first introduced in Europe, overnight mail services (Federal Express,

DHL, UPS) were thought to be scandalous. They were declared illegal because they challenged the monopoly of government mail services.

Then people realized that replacing a monopoly with competition benefited both the company and the customer, who is assured of better service for the price. Hundreds of new jobs were created. Express couriers are now well accepted in Europe, as they are in almost all countries.

Lobbies against network marketing have been established by individuals and companies whose businesses are affected by its success. The network marketing approach to marketing challenges the classical method of selling and advertising. People involved in traditional distribution are frightened of losing their power.

Does this mean network marketing is harmful to society as a whole? What if network marketing offers a solution to the economic crisis by offering a business whose full potential is yet to be realized?

$$*$$

## Network Marketing and the Fear of Loss

Entrepreneurship involves taking risks. Often this means financial risk, but it can also lead to lost time and wasted energy if there are no positive results. In every case, however, regardless of the end result, one will always gain something from the experience: knowledge, a better understanding of ourselves and others, and so on.

Network marketing involves only minimal financial risk and does not force us to give up our regular job. We can devote as much time as we choose to it.

The real risk involved in network marketing is finding out if we have what it takes to succeed. It is a profession very different from any other, so it does not matter how many letters we have after our name. We still have to start from scratch to learn the business and to be on an equal footing with other distributors. We risk comparison with others and rewards only for our profitable results. Not everyone can stretch their "comfort zone" and do what it takes to overcome their limiting beliefs.

Yet this is another reason why network marketing is such an opportunity! Those who feel capable of succeeding have everything within their grasp.

*

## Network Marketing Seen through the Media's Pessimistic Looking Glass

Why do journalists report negative aspects of this flourishing industry? Why do they put the public on guard against products of excellent quality?

Journalists address themselves to their audience. Who is their audience? For the most part it is the group of slow adaptors and cautious people, delighted to have their fears confirmed "in writing."

Nevertheless, we are now approaching the phase of acceptance. Newspapers are starting to write positive articles on this means of distribution. The *Wall Street Journal* even published an article entitled, "Visions of Wealth and Independence Lead Professional to Try Multi-Level" in its June 23, 1995, edition.

# Conclusion

Faith Popcorn states that in order to be successful an enterprise or idea must sooner or later satisfy the trends of American life.

Network marketing undeniably corresponds to most of the trends establishing themselves in different parts of the world today. Trends usually last a minimum of 10 years, which leads one to believe that network marketing will develop tremendously to become a common distribution method in a few years' time.

As powerful as it is, network marketing can only be effective when it offers goods and services that meet consumer demands. Considering the increasing frequency of innovation and the growing popularity and success of network marketing, there is a very good chance that manufacturers will look more and more to this distribution method to bring their products to the market.

Tomorrow's technologies promise to enhance the efficiency of the network marketing system. Visual conferencing will certainly help in organizing meetings and trainings in people's homes.

Furthermore, shopping through multimedia systems is certainly going to develop in the near future. Network marketing will help the client make decisions when the role of the distributor evolves into making recommendations and answering questions.

The world is in a state of accelerated evolution. New opportunities arise every day, and network marketing is one of them. It is not the solution to all of society's problems—unemployment, stress, conflicts at home and in the office. However, network marketing is one solution, and it has the advantage of being well within the grasp of anyone who wants it.

Clearly, network marketing is set to succeed and its future is bright!

✳

# Appendix A

# Trends Identified by Faith Popcorn's BrainReserve

1. Cocooning: The stay-at-home trend, reflecting our strong desire to build soft and cozy nests in order to protect ourselves from the harsh, unpredictable realities of the outside world.

2. Clanning: The inclination to join up, belong to, hang out with groups of like kinds, providing a secure feeling that our own belief system will somehow be validated by consensus.

3. Fantasy Adventure: As a break from modern tensions, we actively seek excitement in basically risk-free adventures, whether via travel, food, movies or virtual reality.

4. Pleasure Revenge: Consumers, tired of all the rules and regulations, want to cut loose and have secret bacchanals with a bevy of forbidden fruits.

5. Anchoring: A new trend that tracks the recent phenomenon of reaching back to our spiritual roots, taking what was

comforting from the past in order to be securely anchored in the future.

6. Egonomics: In a direct reaction to the sterile computer era, we are looking for new ways to make more-personal statements. Thus, business that market to the "I" and provide exceptional service should excel.

7. FemaleThink: A trend that reflects a new set of business and societal values, encouraging us to shift marketing consciousness from the traditional goal-oriented, hierarchical models to the more caring and sharing, familial ones.

8. Mancipation: A NewThink for men that goes beyond being "strictly business" and warmly embraces the freedom of being and individual.

9. 99 Lives: A new look at the modern motto of "Too Fast a Pace, Too Little Time," which forces us all to assume multiple roles in order to cope with busy, high-tech lives.

10. Cashing Out: Working women and men, questioning the intrinsic value of a high-powered career, are opting for more fulfillment in a simpler way of living.

11. Being Alive: There's a growing awareness that a new concept of "wellness" can add generous years of good health, giving us an overall better quality to our lives.

12. Down-Aging: Nostalgia for a carefree childhood lets us introduce a new sense of lightness into our often-too-serious adult lives.

13. Vigilante Consumer: A scanning of the various ways the frustrated, often angry consumer can manipulate the marketplace through pressure, protest and politics.

14. Icon Toppling: A new socioquake has transformed mainstream America and the world, forcing us to question and often reject our monuments of business/government, the long-accepted "pillars of society."

15. S.O.S. (Save Our Society): In order to protect our endangered planet, we must rediscover a social conscience based on a necessary blend of ethics, passion and compassion.

✳

# Appendix B

# The 10 Megatrends According to the John Naisbitt Group

In 1982, Naisbitt identified the following trends in his first book, *Megatrends*:

**1.** From an industrial society to an informational society.
**2.** From a technological base to selective, high technology.
**3.** From domestic economics to planetary economics.
**4.** From short-term to long-term.
**5.** From centralization to decentralization.
**6.** From assistance to the individual's making it on his own.
**7.** From democratic representation to democratic participation.
**8.** From hierarchy to networking.
**9.** From North to South.
**10.** From yes-no decision to multiple choice.

In his second work, in collaboration with Patricia Aburdene and titled *Megatrends 2000*, he notes the following trends:

1. The global economy.
2. Renaissance of the arts.
3. Liberal socialism.
4. Global lifestyle and cultural nationalism.
5. Privatization of the public sector.
6. Emergence of peaceful zone.
7. Arrival of the power of women.
8. Biologic age.
9. Religious renewal.
10. Triumph of the individual.

\*

# Appendix C

# Changes According to Denis Waitley

In *Empires of the Mind*, Denis Waitley defines the following societal shifts.

Yesterday natural resources defined power.
Today knowledge is power.

Yesterday hierarchy was the model.
Today synergy is the mandate.

Yesterday leaders commanded and controlled.
Today leaders empower and coach.

Yesterday leaders were warriors.
Today leaders are facilitators.

Yesterday leaders demanded respect.
Today leaders encourage self-respect.

Yesterday shareholders came first.
Today customers come first.

Yesterday managers directed.
Today managers delegate.

Yesterday supervisors flourished.
Today supervisors vanish.

Yesterday employees took orders.
Today teams make decisions.

Yesterday seniority signified status.
Today creativity drives process.

Yesterday production determined availability.
Today quality determines demand.

Yesterday value was extra.
Today value is everything.

Yesterday everyone was a competitor.
Today everyone is a customer.

Yesterday profits were earned through expediency.
Today profits are earned with integrity.

\*

# Bibliography

Barker, Joel Arthur. *Future Edge, Discovering the New Paradigms of Success*. New York: William Morrow and Company Inc., 1992.

Berger, Jon. The *Manual of Multi-Level Selling Law*. Farnham: Skilfu Publishing, 1991.

Bodnar, Janet. "How TV Sees the Economy". *Changing Times*, December, 1989.

Centre des Jeunes Dirigeants. *Construire le travail de demain*. Paris: Editions d'organisations, 1995.

Cheung, Steven. "Ronald Harry Coase," *The New Palgrave: A Dictionary of Economics*. London: MacMillan Press, 1987.

Clothier, Peter. *Multi-Level Marketing*. London: Kogan Page, 1992.

Conn, Charles Paul. *Promises to Keep*. New York: Berkeley Books, 1985.

Engelhart, W.H. Prof. Dr. *Definition and Volume of Direct Selling of Goods and Services to Consumers*, Research Study of Ruhr University of Bochum. Germany: unpublished, 1992.

Failla, Don. *Ten Napkins Presentation*. USA: Joe Chardwick, 1984.

Hitching, Francis. *Boom Business of the Nineties*. Manchester: MPG Publications, 1993.

Kalench, John. *Being the Best You Can Be in MLM*. San Diego: MIM Publications, 1988.

Katz, Elihy and Paul F. Lazarsfeld. *Personal Influence*. New York: The Free Press, 1955.

Kotler, Philip and Bernard Dubois. *Marketing Management*. Paris: Publi Union, 1994.

Masurel, Jacques. *La vente multi-niveaux*. Fernay-Voltaire: Interconcept, 1994.

Naisbitt, John. *Megatrends*. New York: Warner, 1982.

Naisbitt, John. *Global Paradox*. London: Nicholas Breatley Publishing, 1995.

Naisbitt, John and Patricia Aburdene. *Megatrends 2000*. New York: Avon Books, 1990.

Nichol, Malcolm J. *The Network Strategy*. Aston Clinton: Uni-Vite Nutrition Ltd, 1989.

Pilzer, Paul Zane. *Unlimited Wealth.* New York: Crown Publishers, 1990.

Pilzer, Paul Zane and Mark and Renee Reid Yarnell. *Should You Quit Before You're Fired?* Carson City: Quantum Leap, 1992.

Popcorn, Faith. *The Popcorn Report.* London: Arrow Books Ltd, 1991.

Popcorn, Faith and Lys Marigold. *Clicking.* New York: HarperCollins Publishers, Inc, 1996.

Rogers Everett. *Diffusion of Innovations.* New York: The Free Press, 1983.

Schreiter, Tom. *Big Al Tells All.* Houston: Kass Publishing, 1985.

Toffler, Alvin. *The Third Wave.* London: Pan Books, 1980.

Toffler, Alvin. *Powership.* New York: Bantam Books, 1990.

Toffler, Alvin and Heidi. *Creating a New Civilization: The Politics of the Third Wave.* Washington, Atlanta: Prayers and Freedom Foundation, 1994.

Waitley, Denis. *Empires of the Mind.* London: Nicholas Breatley Publishing, 1995.